D1258197

Let's Play Tag!

⬛ Read the Page

▶ Read the Story

🔄 Repeat

⬛ Stop

⭐ Game

★ Level 1   ★★ Level 2   ★★★ Level 3

💻

PIRATES!

The Treasure of Turtle Island

written by Scott Sonneborn

illustrated by Bill Mudron

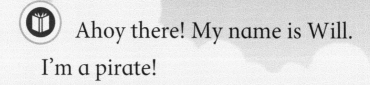 Ahoy there! My name is Will.
I'm a pirate!

Captain Bartholomew Blackhawk
and Iron Katie are my parents.
My sister Abigail and I are part
of their pirate crew.

One day, Abby and I were up in the crow's nest. She saw something floating in the water. "Avast! There's a map in that bottle," she said.

"A *treasure* map!"

Just then, a mean old pirate named
One Tooth sailed up in his sloop.

"I'll be taking that map," he shouted.
"But first, I'll send the lot of you to
Davy Jones' locker!"

One Tooth fired his cannons.
We were under attack!

"We can't let that scallywag get the
map," said Abby. "We saw it first!"

So we grabbed it
before One Tooth could.

Mom threw a stinkpot on One Tooth's ship. He was too busy holding his nose to stop us from sailing away.

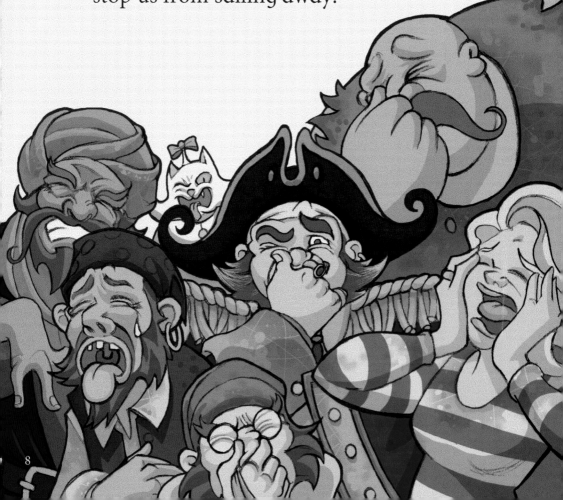

I looked at the map.

"Arrrr!" I grumbled. "How are we going to find the treasure? There's no 'X' on this map!"

The only thing written on it was a pirate song.

"Maybe we should sing the song," Abigail said. So we did.

If you want to get my treasure chest

Sail for Turtle Island to the west.

♪ You'll find my gold buried
under the purple palm tree.

But beware—under the rock,
a trapped chest there be! ♪

I pointed at the map. There was
an island that looked like a turtle!

 We sailed to the island.
But One Tooth followed us!

While mom and dad fought his crew,
One Tooth jumped onto the beach.

That greedy freebooter was going to get the treasure. Unless my sister and I got it first!

 But before we could, One Tooth grabbed us!

"Let go, you scurvy dog!" Abby yelled.

"Yo ho no!" said One Tooth. "I need you swabbies to tell me what the map said. Where be the treasure?"

The song on the map said there was a
trap under the rock. So that's where I told
One Tooth to dig!

But just like the song said, it was a **trap!**

"Arrr! You bilge rats hornswoggled me!"
cried One Tooth.

Abigail and I dug up the treasure chest. It was full of gold doubloons.

Mom and Dad came to help us carry it back.

"Ready to sail for another adventure, matey?" my sister asked.

"Aye Aye!" I said with a smile.

cap

can

man

gap

mad

tap

fad

cape

cane

mane

gape

made

tape

fade

19

hay   mail

nail   pail

chain   tray

bay   pay

            tail

ai

n
ch
p h
t r
m
t
b

ai
ay

l
n

ay

dry

bunny

cry

funny

puppy

kitty

sunny

sky

fry

fly

cry	sunny
fly	funny
dry	puppy
fry	kitty
sky	bunny

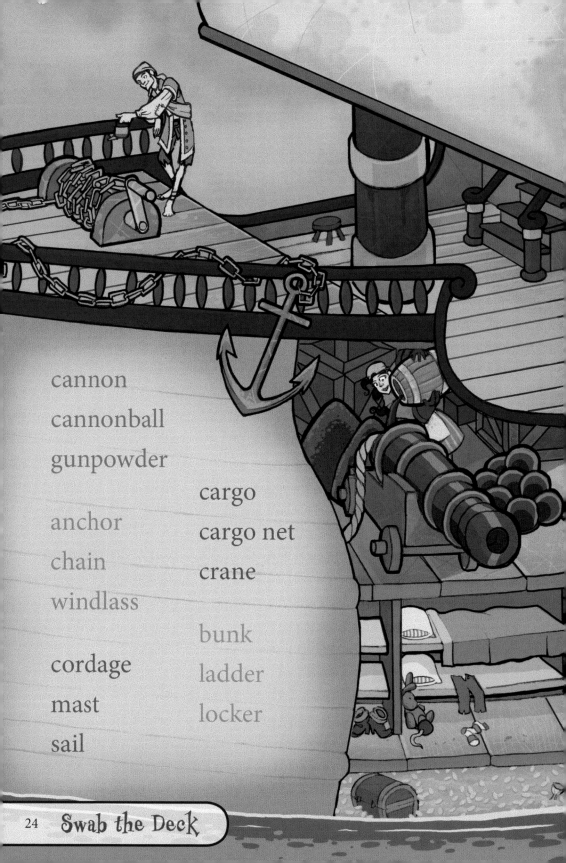

cannon

cannonball

gunpowder

        cargo

anchor   cargo net

chain   crane

windlass

        bunk

cordage   ladder

mast   locker

sail